Librarian

Lucy M. George

AndoTwin

Rita is a librarian. She loves working at the library.

Lots of people visit every day to learn something new, research something old, or to read for fun.

Today is a very special day. The library is
five years old, which means they are having a...

...party!

The library is full of people
who have come to celebrate.

Lots of children have arrived for Story Time, but Rita notices a boy who doesn't want to come in.

"I don't like books," he tells Rita.

"Oh," says Rita. "Well, do you like parties?"

Evan nods.

"What's in the box, Rita?" asks Pat,
one of the other librarians.

"It's a surprise!"
says Rita.

"Why don't you join us?
We are reading all about
parties today."

"Does anyone else like parties?"
she asks. "YES!" they all
shout, and Rita laughs.

First, Rita reads a book about a grumpy dinosaur who doesn't want a party for her birthday.

Then she reads a book about a fancy dress party where all the costumes come to life.

Finally, she reads a book about a surprise birthday party.

"Do any of you like surprises?" Rita asks the children.

"YES!" they cry.

Rita goes over to the cupboard and takes out the hidden box.

"Surprise!" Rita shouts.

Everybody sings:

"Happy birthday to you!

Happy birthday to you!

Happy birthday
dear library!

Happy birthday to you!"

"Can you help me blow
the candles out?" says Rita.

With a big puff, they blow all the
candles out, just like the characters
in the books they read earlier.

Rita cuts the
cake and gives
everyone a piece.
Evan loves cake.

After the cake,
Rita helps the
children find books
about things they
like. Evan wants
to go home.

"What's your favorite thing, Evan?" Rita asks.

"Rocket ships,"
says Evan.

Rita has an idea. "Come with me!"

Rita finds a book with a
huge pop-out rocket ship!

All the children gather around to take a look. Evan holds the book and turns the pages while Rita reads the words.

The book tells them all about planets, stars, meteorites, moons, satellites, and rockets!

Evan loves the book! He's learned a lot, especially about rockets and satellites going around the Earth.

"Wow!" says Evan, turning the pages.

"This is amazing."

"I'm going to find you some more books about space!" says Rita.

"Thank you!" says Evan.

Rita helps Evan scan his books so that he can borrow them from the library.

"See you next time!" says Rita, smiling.

"Bye, Rita! And happy birthday, library!" says Evan.

What else does Rita do?

Puts books away and keeps the shelves in order.

Orders new books.

Helps people use the computers.

Finds books for people.

What does Rita need?

Knowledge about books!

Computer

Nametag

Scanner

Keys for the library

Other busy people

Here are some of the other busy people librarians work with.

Authors write stories and books with lots of facts. They visit libraries to talk to children and adults about the books they write.

Support workers care for and help people with learning difficulties or physical disabilities.

Teachers plan school visits to the library so children can choose books they would like to borrow.

Parents/Caregivers visit libraries with their children to borrow books, visit authors, use the computers, or for activities like Story Time.

Classroom Connections

- Ask the children if they knew what a librarian was before they read the book? Do they know any librarians? Discuss what a librarian does.

- In the story, Evan said he didn't like books. In the end he discovered some that he loved. What made him like books? Have the children ever thought they didn't like something, and then found out they did after all?

- Evan liked the books about space best. What books do the children like best? Do they have a favorite author, illustrator, or character? What is their favorite book at the moment?

- In the story, the library had a party. Rita organized a surprise. Ask the children if they like surprises? What's the best surprise they can think of?

- Libraries contain books on almost anything you can think of. As a game, ask the children to suggest some things they'd like to make a book about, and then make up titles for these books. Then, as a follow-up activity help the children to make the books.

Quarto is the authority on a wide range of topics.

Quarto educates, entertains and enriches the lives of our readers—enthusiasts and lovers of hands-on living.

www.quartoknows.com

Editor: Sophie Hallam
Designer: Victoria Kimonidou

Copyright © QEB Publishing 2017

First Published in the US in 2017 by
QEB Publishing
Part of The Quarto Group
6 Orchard, Lake Forest, CA 92630

A CIP record for this book is available from the Library of Congress.

ISBN 978 1 68297 135 2

Printed in China

For Granny Wilson

- AndoTwin

For Emily, Jessica, Isabella & Evie

- Lucy M. George